WALKIN

BRON**te** WAY

HILLSIDE GUIDES - ACROSS THE NORTH & BEYOND

The Uplands of Britain
- **THE HIGH PEAKS OF ENGLAND & WALES**
- **YORKSHIRE DALES, MOORS & FELLS**

Long Distance Walks

•COAST TO COAST WALK	•DALES WAY	•CLEVELAND WAY
•WESTMORLAND WAY	•FURNESS WAY	•CUMBERLAND WAY
•BRONTE WAY	•PENDLE WAY	•NIDDERDALE WAY
•LADY ANNE'S WAY	•TRANS-PENNINE WAY	•CALDERDALE WAY

Hillwalking - Lake District
- **LAKELAND FELLS - SOUTH**   •LAKELAND FELLS - EAST
- **LAKELAND FELLS - NORTH**   •LAKELAND FELLS - WEST

Circular Walks - Peak District
- **NORTHERN PEAK**   •EASTERN PEAK   •CENTRAL PEAK
- **SOUTHERN PEAK**   •WESTERN PEAK

Circular Walks - Yorkshire Dales
- **HOWGILL FELLS**   •THREE PEAKS   •MALHAMDALE
- **WHARFEDALE**   •NIDDERDALE   •WENSLEYDALE   •SWALEDALE

Circular Walks - North York Moors
- **WESTERN MOORS**   •SOUTHERN MOORS   •NORTHERN MOORS

Circular Walks - South Pennines
- **BRONTE COUNTRY**   •ILKLEY MOOR
- **CALDERDALE**   •SOUTHERN PENNINES

Circular Walks - Lancashire
- **BOWLAND**   •PENDLE & THE RIBBLE   •WEST PENNINE MOORS

Circular Walks - North Pennines
- **TEESDALE**   •EDEN VALLEY

Yorkshire Pub Walks
- **HARROGATE/WHARFE VALLEY**   •HAWORTH/AIRE VALLEY

- **YORKSHIRE DALES CYCLE WAY**   •WEST YORKSHIRE CYCLE WAY
- **MOUNTAIN BIKING - WEST & SOUTH YORKSHIRE**
- **AIRE VALLEY BIKING GUIDE**   •CALDERDALE BIKING GUIDE
- **GLASGOW Clyde Valley & Loch Lomond (Biking)**

- **YORK WALKS**   *City Theme Walks*

Send for a detailed current catalogue and pricelist

WALKING COUNTRY

BRONTË WAY

Paul Hannon

HILLSIDE

HILLSIDE
PUBLICATIONS
12 Broadlands
Shann Park
Keighley
West Yorkshire
BD20 6HX

First published 2000

© Paul Hannon 2000

ISBN 1 870141 56 3

Whilst the author has walked and researched the entire route for the purposes of this guide, no responsibility can be accepted for any unforeseen circumstances encountered while following it. The publisher would, however, greatly appreciate any information regarding material changes, and any problems encountered.

Cover illustrations:
The Worth Valley at Ponden; Watersheddles waymark
Back cover: Near Gawthorpe Hall, looking to Pendle Hill
(Paul Hannon/Big Country Picture Library)

Page One: Main Street, Haworth
Page Three: At the Brontë Parsonage, Haworth

Printed in Great Britain by
Carnmor Print
95-97 London Road
Preston
Lancashire
PR1 4BA

CONTENTS

Wycoller Hall

INTRODUCTION

The Brontë Way is a 45 mile walk combining countless links with the celebrated literary family of that name. The route stretches from Oakwell Hall near Birstall, in Yorkshire, to Gawthorpe Hall, near Padiham in Lancashire. Despite the exemplary theme, walkers with absolutely no interest in the Brontës will still find this a fascinating and thoroughly enjoyable walk.

The original Brontë Way was devised in 1985 as a simple 9 mile walk between Wycoller and Haworth, promoted largely by Lancashire County Council. Only later was the theme developed to incorporate a rich assortment of buildings and locations with Brontë associations, and in 1993 a new, greatly extended route was declared open. The project was implemented through the Standing Conference of South Pennine Authorities (SCOSPA), a group of local authorities and other interested bodies actively and sensitively promoting the whole South Pennine area. This unified approach is highlighted by the fact that the walk passes through the patches of Kirklees, Calderdale, Bradford, Pendle and Burnley councils.

The route of the Way embraces a remarkable variety of surroundings from canal towpath to windswept moor, including historic fieldpaths linking old textile settlements, and surprising wooded valleys so near urban communities, such as Coley Beck and Thursden Brook. The central section crosses the backbone of England, the Pennine watershed linking Yorkshire and Lancashire. These moorland miles can be extended to bring in memorable detours, notably to the atmospheric setting of Top Withins (the commonly enduring image of Emily's *Wuthering Heights*), and also to the bristly crest of Boulsworth Hill, perhaps the Way's finest landmark.

Getting around
The Way is ideally placed for walking in separate day sections, with many West Yorkshire and East Lancashire conurbations close to hand. There are ample bus services at numerous points along the way, including the termini of each stage (the start and finish points are just a short walk along their respective driveways from main roads). The main exception is Wycoller, which is, however, conveniently served by a short linking path to/from the main road at Laneshaw Bridge.

Using the guide

The main section of the guide is a detailed description of the route and its associated features. Divided into four manageable sections, each offers a steady ramble with good or easily arranged transport links. A compromise for strong walkers would be to spend a strenuous weekend over it, but even then, some features of interest would be missed in the desire to tick the miles off.

Each of the four stages is self-contained, with essential information being followed by a simple map and a concise route description. Dovetailed in between are notes of features along the way, and interspersed are illustrations which capture the flavour of the walk and document many items of interest. Essential route description has been highlighted in bold, in order to make it easily accessible in amongst the other snippets of information. The sketch maps serve only to identify the location of the route, and whilst the description should be sufficient to guide one around, an Ordnance Survey map is strongly recommended.

The entire route is covered by just two maps at the 1:25,000 scale:
- Explorer 288 - *Bradford & Huddersfield*
- Outdoor Leisure 21 - *South Pennines*

They are indispensible companions to the guidebook, as both have the route highlighted (though the first edition of the Explorer map, published in 1999, curiously declines to highlight the initial 3 miles of the Way). Additionally, at the 1:50,000 scale, the route is covered by:
- Landranger 103 - *Blackburn & Burnley*
- Landranger 104 - *Leeds, Bradford & Harrogate*

These are particularly useful for general planning purposes.

For much of the walk, the Brontë Way's own signs (a yellow arrow on a magenta background) are prevalent, and these are often found in unlikely and sometimes easily missed locations. Many sections are without them however: mostly, but not always, when the Way overlaps with several other 'named' walks, namely the Kirklees Way, Spen Way/Spen Valley Heritage Trail, Calderdale Way, Pendle Way and Burnley Way. Invariably these other routes' waymarks take precedence when met by the Brontë Way.

Pages 10 and 11 offer a brief look at the Brontë family.

SOME USEFUL FACILITIES

A general guide only

	Youth Hostel	Accommodation	Bus service	Rail station	Pub	Post office	Other shop	WC	Phone	Cafe
Birstall		•	•		•	•	•	•	•	•
Oakwell Hall		•					•	•	•	•
Gomersal		•	•	•	•				•	•
Rawfolds		•						•	•	
Hightown		•			•	•	•		•	
Hartshead		•			•				•	
Clifton	•	•			•	•		•	•	
Brighouse	•	•	•	•	•	•	•	•	•	•
Bailiff Bridge		•			•	•		•	•	
Norwood Green		•			•				•	
Shelf	•	•			•	•	•	•	•	
Clayton Heights		•			•	•	•	•	•	
Thornton	•	•			•	•	•	•	•	•
Well Heads		•			•				•	
Keelham		•			•				•	•
Denholme Gate		•								
Leeming	•	•							•	
Oxenhope	•	•	•		•	•		•	•	•
Marsh	•	•							•	
Haworth	•	•	•	•	•	•	•	•	•	•
Stanbury	•	•			•				•	
Ponden	•	•								•
Wycoller	•							•		•
Laneshaw Bridge	•	•			•	•	•			
Trawden	•	•			•	•	•	•	•	•
Swinden Bridge					•					
Worsthorne		•			•				•	•
Burnley	•	•	•	•	•	•	•	•	•	•
Habergham		•			•	•	•		•	
Gawthorpe Hall		•					•	•		•
Rose Grove		•	•	•				•		
Padiham	•	•			•	•	•	•	•	•

SOME USEFUL ADDRESSES

Ramblers' Association
2nd Floor, Camelford House, 87-89 Albert Embankment, London SE1 7BR
Tel. 020-7339 8500

Rights of Way/Countryside Officers
Kirklees Tel. 01484-225575   **Calderdale** Tel. 01422-359454
Bradford Tel. 01535-618300   **Pendle** Tel. 01282-661661
Burnley Tel. 01282-425011

Lancashire Countryside Service
PO Box 9, Guild House, Cross Street, Preston PR1 8RD
Tel. 01772-264709

Information
3-5 Albion Street, **Huddersfield** Tel. 01484-430808
Piece Hall, **Halifax** Tel. 01422-368725
Central Library, Prince's Way, **Bradford** Tel. 01274-753678
2-4 West Lane, **Haworth** Tel. 01535-642329
Wycoller Country Park, **Wycoller** Tel. 01282-870253
Pendle Heritage Centre, Park Hill, **Barrowford** Tel. 01282-661701
Town Hall, Market Street, **Nelson** Tel. 01282-661655
County Information Centre, Bus Station, **Nelson** Tel. 01282-698533
Burnley Mechanics, Manchester Road, **Burnley** Tel. 01282-664421
County Information Centre, Bus Station, **Burnley** Tel. 01282-423125

Public Transport
Metro (West Yorkshire buses and trains) Tel. 0113-245 7676
Lancashire County Transport Information   Tel. 01772-254868
National Rail Enquiry Line Tel. 0345-484950

The Brontë Society
Brontë Parsonage, Haworth, Keighley BD22 8DR Tel. 01535-642323

Places of interest open to visitors
Oakwell Hall, Birstall   Tel. 01924-326240
The Red House, Gomersal   Tel. 01274-335100
Brontë Birthplace, Thornton   Tel. 01274-830849
Brontë Parsonage, Haworth   Tel. 01535-642323
Keighley & Worth Valley Railway   Tel. 01535-645214
          24-hour Timetable/Information Service: 01535-647777
Gawthorpe Hall, Padiham   Tel. 01282-771004

THE BRONTËS

Patrick Brunty was born in 1777, eldest of 10 children raised in conditions of hardship in County Down. Through a fortunate acquaintance he had the opportunity to study at Cambridge, and he amended his name in recognition of his hero Lord Nelson (who had become Duke of Brontë). After a spell in southern England he came north to Yorkshire, initially to Dewsbury. He began his curacy at Hartshead in 1811, and lodged at a nearby farm. The following year he married Maria Branwell, a Cornishwoman, and they took up residence at Clough House, Hightown. Here their first two children, Maria and Elizabeth, were born.

In 1815 Brontë moved to Thornton, though the Bell Chapel is now merely a few remains in the shadow of the later church. In a small house in the village street the remaining four children were born, Charlotte in 1816, Patrick Branwell in 1817, Emily Jane in 1818, and Anne in 1820. No sooner was the family complete then it was on the move again, this time to their celebrated home, the parsonage at Haworth. Here all but one of them were to end their lives, indeed the children lost their mother the very next year. The death of the elder daughters in 1825 left the four other children to attain adulthood.

The three sisters departed on numerous occasions to spend largely unsuccessful spells as teachers and governesses in other parts of the region, while Branwell, the only brother, showed promise as an artist. His progress, however, soon faltered, and after a spell as a railway clerk at Luddenden Foot, in the Calder Valley, he returned home: stricken by illness he saw out his closing years as a regular of the Black Bull, adjacent to the church. Meanwhile the sisters had also returned to the fold, but in their cases to begin their pitifully short literary careers. In an age when such activity by women was frowned upon, the sisters' first works appeared under the pseudonyms Currer, Ellis and Acton Bell, with each retaining their initials.

When the first novels were published Emily and Anne had little time to enjoy any acclaim, for their deaths rapidly followed the demise of Branwell in 1848. Anne was buried in Scarborough, where the sea air had offered no escape from the common killer tuberculosis, then known as consumption, that accounted for all but Charlotte. Charlotte's first published novel *Jane Eyre* was followed by further works, during which time she enjoyed critical acclaim and popularity. She even survived long enough to marry her father's curate, the Rev. Arthur Bell Nicholls in 1854, though tragically her flame was also to burn out the very next year, still not 39. Thus Patrick Brontë was to outlive all his children, attaining the ripe old age of 84.

What makes the story of the Brontë sisters so memorable is the nature of the background to their literary achievements, notably the adversity the family had faced, and more appreciably still the brooding mass of moorland beyond their Haworth home, where they sought and found untold inspiration. Listed is a chronology of the novels' publication.

1847
Jane Eyre (Charlotte)
Wuthering Heights (Emily)
Agnes Grey (Anne)
1848
The Tenant of Wildfell Hall (Anne)
1849
Shirley (Charlotte)
1853
Villette (Charlotte)
1857
The Professor (Charlotte)

Haworth Parsonage

STAGE 1

OAKWELL HALL TO SHELF

Distance: 10½ miles/17km

Map:
1:50,000
Landranger 104 - Leeds, Bradford & Harrogate
1:25,000
Explorer 288 - Bradford & Huddersfield

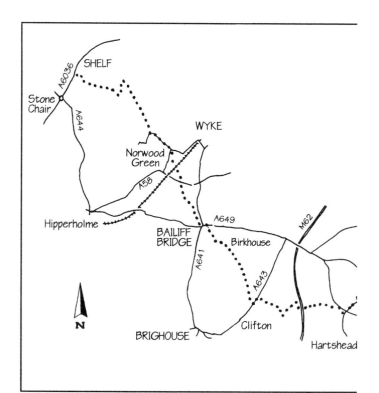

➡ **The Brontë Way begins at Oakwell Hall, off the A652 Bradford-Dewsbury road, between Birkenshaw and Birstall.** This Elizabethan manor house (illustrated overleaf) was built by the Batt family, and visitors can enter within its sombre gritstone walls to glimpse the lifestyle of a well-to-do family of that period. Charlotte Brontë visited when it was a girls' school, and featured it as Fieldhead in *Shirley*. Now managed by Kirklees Council, it is at the heart of a country park in the shadow of the M62. Other features are an information centre, cafe, shop and nature trail. In June 1643 the Battle of Adwalton Moor was fought less than a mile to the north, with the Parliamentarian forces having to retreat along Warren's Lane past Oakwell Hall. Both the hall and grounds are open throughout the year.

Before commencing, note that the 1999 Explorer map fails to highlight the opening 3 miles of the Brontë Way as far as Rawfolds (our route shouldn't be confused with that of the Spen Way/Spen Valley Heritage Trail). From the front of the hall, head down the short drive to the car park entrance and the gates onto a minor road.

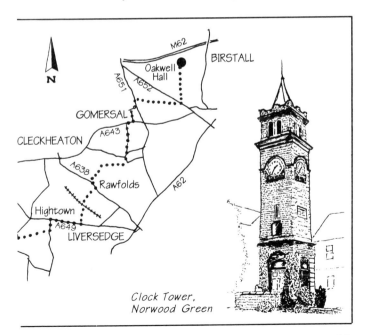

Clock Tower,
Norwood Green

Cross straight over past a house, and a broad path descends the fieldside to a stone bridge accessing the A652 Bradford-Dewsbury road. En route, the solid tower of St. Peter's church, Birstall can clearly be seen. Rebuilt since the Brontës' time, it was Briarfield church in *Shirley*. Here is buried Ellen Nussey, a schoolfriend of Charlotte's who lived nearby, and remained a close friend until Charlotte's death.

Oakwell Hall

Cross straight over the road and along suburban Monk Ings. As the road swings round to the right, take a rough road branching left between houses. At the end a stile by the gate ahead sends a faint path off across the field. The way rises gently through the fields amidst a haven of greenery. At the end of the second field, note the benchmark on the big stone post. There is no escaping the sight and sound of the motorway over to the right. Rising further, bear right towards a clump of trees, with an old iron kissing-gate beneath. A stone post bears another benchmark.

The briefly enclosed path runs left, with a sports field just over the hedge. The path then runs by the wall enclosing a burial ground to join a drive, going left through a small corner of modern housing and out onto the A651 Bradford-Heckmondwike road at Gomersal. Cross and turn left to Gomersal Public Hall, then into the car park at the rear of the Red House. Dating from 1660, the Red House is named from its bright, red-brick exterior in an otherwise stone-built district. Charlotte regularly visited Mary Taylor (they became friends while at Roe Head School in Mirfield) and her family here, and the house featured as Briarmains in *Shirley*. Today this too is owned by Kirklees Council, and is open to the public as a museum in the flavour of the Taylor's and Brontë era.

Cross the grassy area behind the car park to a wall-gap into a snicket in front of a large works. This vast building shares with the Red House its red brickwork, if little else! **Go left along this long, tightly enclosed footway to emerge onto the A643 Cleckheaton-Birstall road almost opposite Gomersal churchyard. Cross and go right to the far end then first left along Shirley Road.** The churchyard path offers an alternative short-cut to the front and out via a gate at the far corner, with far-reaching views to the west. St. Mary's is a large, imposing building with a fine west tower. Mary Taylor's gravestone can be seen on the western side, by the churchyard wall.

Go left along Shirley Road, straight over a roundabout and passing the length of the Shirley housing estate. The branch streets also recall Charlotte's heroine: small wonder that this opening area of the walk has been dubbed Shirley Country. **At the end the road narrows into a contrastingly attractive way, dropping down to emerge onto Upper Lane.** Just 50 yards to the right, the *Wheatsheaf* pub stands across a broad road junction. **The way crosses straight over Upper Lane and into the open field below, dropping all the way down its side to leave by a gap at the bottom corner. Turn right past Gomersal Lodge, along Lower Lane.** Note the dignified red-brick residences of Sisters' Houses, where the Misses Wooler lived. They ran Roe Head School at Mirfield, where Charlotte both learnt and later taught. Margaret Wooler gave Charlotte away at her marriage.

As the road swings up to the right, take a short snicket on the left, squeezing between gardens to emerge at a pair of stiles at a field corner. This is a glorious moment, trading suburbia for spacious views over the Spen Valley to the Calder Valley and the massive Emley Moor TV mast. Further right are the rolling moors and shapely nabs of the north-eastern corner of the Peak District National Park, above and beyond Meltham. Dwarfed beneath the skyline is the tower on Castle Hill, above Almondbury, Huddersfield.

Advance along the field top path, a grand stroll that continues across a field centre to a stile onto a farm track. Continue straight ahead, on the track that has deposed what was until recently a splendid enclosed pathway. At the end, bear left across the open field,

dropping to a stile onto a stony, enclosed track. Go left, dropping to a corner, the site of Walsh Houses on the map. Descend the wallside to the bottom to enter trees. Crossing a barely discernible old railway line the path drops onto the top of New Street.

Head down New Street to the A638 Cleckheaton-Heckmondwike road at Rawfolds. Cleckheaton is just half a mile to the right. Over the road stood Rawfolds Mill, the scene of riotous activity in April 1812 when Luddites rose up against the introduction of factory machines that threatened their livelihoods. The Spen Valley was very much a hotbed of Luddite activity, and this played a major part in *Shirley*. Charlotte would have gleaned much from first-hand stories from her father, who was curate at nearby Hartshead at the time. Go left as far as Royds Park, a pleasant public park.

Cross the dual carriageway and head directly away along Primrose Lane. The rough road heads on past an athletics stadium, and bridges the river Spen before rising to pass under a defunct railway bridge. This carried the line south from Bradford through Cleckheaton and Heckmondwike, and has very recently been converted to a 'greenway' for the use of walkers and cyclists. The lane swings up again to rise to the edge of modern housing. Pause to look back over the scene so far, and possibly pass some rare farm breeds. Continue up and straight on past the houses, the rough road leading out onto the A649 Halifax-Liversedge road at Hightown, on the edge of Liversedge. On the right is an attractive white-walled cottage with mullioned windows. Just along to the left is the *Shears Inn,* which earned infamy as a Luddite meeting place. Of perhaps equal interest is the presence of a fish & chip shop.

Turn right along the road, a short ten minutes leading on past another pub, the *Cross Keys,* before reaching a shop at a junction with Clough Lane. On the right stands Clough House, a distinguished three-storeyed dwelling to which Patrick Brontë came after his marriage to Maria Branwell in 1812. It was here their first two children, Maria and Elizabeth, were born.

Turn down Clough Lane, leaving the village behind to reach the bridge on Clough Beck at the bottom. Note, on the right, the previous bridge languishing in dense undergrowth. At this point leave the road by doubling back a few yards on the line of the old road, and take a stile by a gate into the field. Rise up the wallside to a small gate in front of a house. A briefly enclosed footway emerges into the yard of Upper House Farm. Praying that the dogs are firmly tethered, head straight along the drive, rising gradually onto a road bend on Hare Park Lane.

Clough House, Hightown

At this point Hartshead church appears directly ahead. Continue straight on. On the left, easily missed, is a small plot of land sheltered by trees, a Quaker burial ground dating from 1665. Four ancient grave slabs mark the resting place of members of the Greene family of Liversedge and a couple of recent additions; a peaceful spot. In the fields over to the right, meanwhile, stands Thorn Bush Farm, where Patrick Brontë first 'lodged' (then as Lousey Thorn Farm) when he became curate at Hartshead in 1811.

Keep straight on to the staggered crossroads with the B6119 Hightown Heights-Hartshead road and along Church Lane towards the church. The route turns right just before it, along Ladywell Road. St. Peter's, Hartshead was restored in 1881, but the hoary tower survives from long before Patrick Brontë's time. This was his first curacy, for five years to 1815, and is a delightful building, low and squat. The seats in the churchyard make a grand spot to halt awhile. Passed en route

17

to the church gate is the abandoned former day school amid gravestones. Across the road stand the old stocks. This hilltop position affords far-reaching views, with Emley Moor looking very close, and Castle Hill, Almondbury now seen in context. The attractive *Gray Ox* pub is just five minutes down the road, with Hartshead village beyond.

St. Peter's, Hartshead

Back on Ladywell Road we now have the company of the Kirklees Way. Turn right at the T-junction at the end, past a few cottages and out along a rough track, Ladywell Lane. At a junction before the main road turn left. This earns a big view west up the Calder Valley, with Ovenden Moor windfarm on the skyline - we'll be almost at the foot of this, some miles hence. **When this farm road turns left to Soap House, take a stile to the right of the gate in front. Walk parallel along the fieldside, at the end rejoining the track, now surfaced. The sound of the imminent M62 is joined by the sight of it, and the track descends to a gas installation.** Further extensive views look ahead up into the folds of Calderdale, while just to our right is Hartshead Moor service area.

A green track continues down to a farm bridge over the motorway. On crossing, reflect that the next motorway crossing, some 37 miles hence, will see the walk almost completed. **Across, turn right down the track, and on a little further to a dip in the golf course.** Walkers still using the old Pathfinder map will find this area unrecognisable. **Turn left at the junction in the dip, and a broad track runs down, largely sheltered from the course to reach a T-junction at the end. Turn right, a broad path widening into a track to lead out through more of the golf course onto the A643 Brighouse-Cleckheaton road.** Brighouse is but a short mile along to the left, beyond Clifton.

Go left on the footway for almost 200 yards, then cross to a stile on the right. Head away along the wall/fence-side, and from the end stile bear right across to some grassy hummocks. These are the remains of Clifton Colliery, and the small bank is a branch from the former mineral tramway whose well-defined embankment is just ahead. The line transported coal down to the valley at Brighouse from workings that were at their peak in the 19th century, though surviving some years into the 20th.

Cross to a stile giving access to the old rail embankment, and straight over it to a stile beneath a tall pylon. Joining a back road (Jay House Lane), take the farm drive opposite (Clough Lane) running on to The Clough. The Kirklees Way takes its leave along here. As the drive swings left for the house, keep on down a few steps to a slab streamlet crossing, and up the gentle rise behind on an obvious line (the abandoned continuation of Clough Lane) towards farm build-ings. Bear left to a stile, and a track leads on past the buildings into Birkhouse.

This attractive hamlet is on the line of an old packhorse route, and Birkhouse Cottage features some mullioned windows. **Advance along the access road.** This emerges with a fine view over Bailiff Bridge, its modern housing clustered around the large carpet factory. In the foreground is another disused railway line. **Descend the road past the appealing Lower Birkhouse Farm, swinging down to absorb the Calderdale Way, with which we share steps as far as Shelf. Either follow the road under the railway, or deviate over the old line to a rough lane, which runs along to rejoin Birkhouse Road. This runs out onto the A649 Halifax-Heckmondwike road.**

Turn left into Bailiff Bridge under two works bridges to the busy crossroads with the A641 Bradford-Brighouse road. Here are shops, toilets and the *Punchbowl* pub. **Cross to the pub and turn right along the street behind, Victoria Road. This ends suddenly just as the factory does, alongside new housing on the right.** This is an unlikely beginning to a magnificent stretch of walking all the way to Shelf.

Keep straight on an inviting green path across open ground, over a small footbridge on Wyke Beck and on to a stile behind. Rise up the hedgeside, and just short of the far end pass through a large gap on the right. Rise up this smaller enclosure with a hedge on the right, and from the stile at the top head up the field centre to a stile onto

the **A58 Leeds-Halifax road alongside a garden centre.** Over to the right stand the forlorn remains of Wyke Viaduct, a tragically abrupt end to the sturdy arches that carried the old line over Wyke Beck.

From a kissing-gate opposite, a path rises up the field towards a railway line. Over to the left, where it bridges the road, note the fading decades-old *Schweppes Table waters* advert. **The path climbs to a grassy stone arched bridge over the Bradford-Halifax railway.** Wyke Tunnel entrance is just along to the right. Pause to look back over the Calder Valley to the Emley Moor mast, while on the near skyline left - looking back - is Wyke church spire. **Across the bridge the path briefly delves into a leafy enclosed way, then runs by an enviably sited cricket pitch and out onto open ground at the edge of Norwood Green. Continue up the track to a road junction behind the war memorial.** The *Pear Tree* pub is just to the right down Station Road.

The Way marches straight up the village street, passing numerous patches of ground that make 'green' a most appropriate name: keep on all the way to a brow at the far end. Several features of interest are passed en route. On the right is the *Old White Beare,* a white-walled pub recalling a ship that helped halt the Spanish Armada. The characterful, low-roofed, multi-roomed interior owes much to its 1590 rebuilding, featuring timbers from the actual ship. St. George's church is passed on the left, soon followed by the United Reformed Church, erected in 1882 as a Congregational Church.

The Old White Beare, Norwood Green

On the very brow, go left a few yards along Chapel Street to see a striking clock tower. The Ellis Memorial Clock Tower was built in 1897, the year of Queen Victoria's Diamond Jubilee. It is now the classy centrepiece of a private garden. In front is another delightful piece of open ground, with seats and daffodils overlooking a big view. **The Way leaves the brow by briefly descending Norwood Green Hill, then turning right along a surfaced road at Lower Ox Heys Farm (now housing). Bear left along the green lane leading to Middle Ox Heys. Here keep straight on to a stile into shrubbery masking the start of a short but charming enclosed pathway.** Coley church tower marks the skyline to the left, above the lovely wooded valley of Coley Beck beneath us.

Emerging at the end in the shadow of a tall pylon, keep on to the next stile from where the path rakes gently down into North Wood. A clear path heads upstream in the tree-lined environs of the beck, featuring a fine waterfall. While springtime bluebells add further character to this delectable wooded dell, the greenery of high summer all but hides the waterfall. **An optional short-cut is available here.**

The main route reaches Dean House as follows: Ignoring branches down to the stream and bridges, keep on above the steep bank as a sunken way rising to the foot of a rough lane. Head up past isolated Heathwood House, and at the bend just above turn left for a steep, stone stepped descent into the trees. Across the simple bridge rise left to a stile above the buildings at Dean House. Better and shorter is the route taking the branch path above the waterfall, dropping to a simple bridge across the beck. Across, a few steps point the way up a steep bank, rising to pass left of the buildings at Dean House. A pair of adjacent stiles lead onto its drive.

However joining the farm drive, turn up it and it leads unfailingly all the way to the A6036 Bradford-Halifax road through Shelf. En route, some good sections of paving of the original road are seen, with grooved centres worn by the passage of wheels. For much of the way there is virtually no evidence of the proximity of civilisation and industry. **Towards the top the old way becomes enclosed, becoming a rough road at Bridle Stile and rising past houses and Shelf Hall Park onto the road.** Approaching the road, note the long attractive stone terrace of Spring Head opposite. Just a minute along to the right is the *Bottomleys Arms* pub.

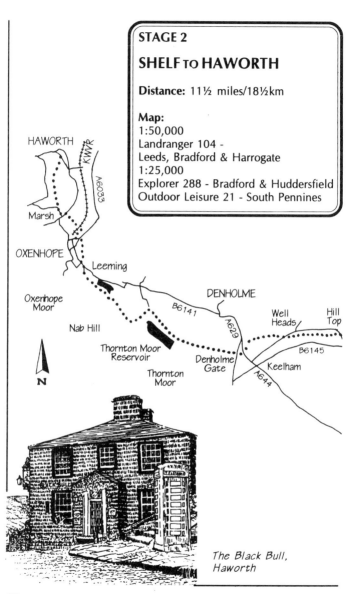

STAGE 2

SHELF TO HAWORTH

Distance: 11½ miles/18½km

Map:
1:50,000
Landranger 104 -
Leeds, Bradford & Harrogate
1:25,000
Explorer 288 - Bradford & Huddersfield
Outdoor Leisure 21 - South Pennines

HAWORTH

KWVR

A6033

Marsh

OXENHOPE

Leeming

DENHOLME

Oxenhope
Moor

B6141

A629

Well
Heads

Hill
Top

Nab Hill

B6145

Thornton Moor
Reservoir

Denholme
Gate

Keelham

N

Thornton
Moor

A644

*The Black Bull,
Haworth*

➡️ **The Way leaves the A6036 at Shelf directly opposite where it entered, passing through a short snicket to emerge onto another road.** If starting from here, the snicket is found at the far end of the long terraced row of Spring Head, on the Halifax side of the *Bottomleys Arms*. **Turn left along the road (Shelf Hall Lane), quickly turning right after Broad Ings Way at a footpath sign pointing along to a farm. Here the Calderdale Way leaves us by remaining on the road.**

Note that an alternative to the sometimes muddy farm environs is available: This turns along Broad Ings Way, and left up Park Stone Rise. At the top a concrete bollard sends a little path between houses to concrete steps over the wall onto a rough field track. Rise left to the main route as it enters the field. **The main route passes to the right of the farm buildings and out along a rough, enclosed way between school grounds and new housing. At the end we emerge into a field.**

Faced by a gate, take the stile alongside and rise to the brow in the company of an old wall. Advance through crumbling walls, an improving track accompanying an improved wall on the right. Over to the left is the noted landmark of Black Dyke Mills chimney at Queensbury. **At the end, the rough road of Bridge Lane is joined**

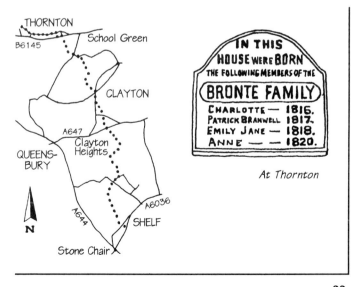

IN THIS
HOUSE WERE BORN
THE FOLLOWING MEMBERS OF THE

BRONTE FAMILY

CHARLOTTE — 1816.
PATRICK BRANWELL 1817.
EMILY JANE — 1818.
ANNE — — 1820.

At Thornton

amid scenes of casual tipping. **Turn right to a road, Giles Hill Lane. Go left a few yards then right along Brackens Lane.** This stage is at quite an altitude, with extensive if unexciting views. The enclosure on the right is occupied by the grassy mounds of old coal workings, this still being known as Coalpit Hills.

At the first opportunity turn left along a short enclosed footway. Emerging into a field, go straight on with the wall on the left, dropping down into a few trees above tiny Blackshaw Beck. Take a stile by a gate on the left and go left on the colourful bank above the stream. Quickly a path drops down to a simple bridge over the beck, then heads steeply up the wall-side. Levelling out, continue on through a stile, with the farm at Bobby Green on the left.

From the next stile slant right to a gap-stile in the rising wall, and head directly away along a wall-side. From the end stile cross to another ahead, then advance to a wall corner in front, this section showing good signs of causeying. Keep on past a few trees to join Stocks Lane alongside a large house. Turn left up here, broadening and rising past a school where it becomes surfaced to meet the A647 Bradford-Halifax road at Clayton Heights by a war memorial. The elevated village of Queensbury is a short mile along to the left.

Go left, briefly. Just a little further is a shop, and just beyond that, the *Old Dolphin Inn*. **The route turns right along Sheep Hill Lane (opposite Chapel Lane which leads to the Methodist Church). The 30mph sign is somewhat superfluous as the rough road quickly narrows into a grand footway descending onto a road.** This enjoys glorious views over the valley towards our objective of Thornton. Further right, above Allerton and the waterworks domes at Chellow Grange, the long skyline of Rombalds Moor can be seen, while a clear day boasts a prospect of Buckden Pike and Great Whernside far up Wharfedale, in the heart of the Yorkshire Dales.

Straight across the road a briefly enclosed path swings left to descend the fieldside to a farm track. Cross straight over and down two further fields to emerge onto Baldwin Lane. Cross and turn right down onto the edge of Clayton. En route, we cross the barely discernible line of the Keighley-Halifax-Bradford railway. Queensbury's triangular station was a good half-mile to the west of this point, yet several hundred feet below the village itself. **At the attractive cottages at Brook Lane, note the carved faces on a stone post. Just a few yards**

further at a junction with Clayton Lane, turn sharp left between houses, and a pleasant enclosed way heads off past the gardens. It runs narrowly on between fields and back gardens to emerge into a field after the last house.

There is now a clearer picture of Thornton just across the valley. **Descend the wallside to the next stile.** On the left is a small quarry site at Hanging Falls. The Thornton picture is further improved, featuring the 20 arches of the mighty Thornton Viaduct. Up to 120ft high, they carried the former Halifax-Bradford-Keighley line across the valley of Pinch Beck. With backing from local industrialists, the line was completed in 1878 by the Great Northern Railway. It was dubbed the 'Alpine Route', such was its situation with viaducts and tunnels through and across the rolling hills and dales. Certainly it was a great engineering feat to bring a railway to this altitude from the surrounding towns. However, the construction and running costs were always a major headache, and the line saw inevitable closure in 1956.

At this T-junction of paths turn sharp right on a path along the field top. At the end, path and wall curve down to a stile by a gate. Once through, ignore the inviting green way heading off, and turn through an old stile and down the wallside. Descend steeply, through a further stile then directly down by the vestiges of a wall to meet a rough track in front of Hole Bottom Beck at the bottom. Turn right on this to a stile onto Low Lane, linking Clayton and Thornton.

Go left, along the one-way section to a T-junction with Chat Hill Road. Turn right briefly, then alongside a house take a cart track running to Corn Mill Farm, whose name tells of its origins. Crossing Pinch Beck keep left of the buildings and advance to a gate, then on a short way to a stile in a wall corner. Rise left towards the waiting church spire, cross one field then climb steeply to an iron kissing-gate in the top corner. Go left a yard or two, then rise up the short rough road past Thornton Hall Farm onto the wide B6145 Bradford-Keelham road through Thornton.

Before crossing, go left a short way to the overgrown churchyard on the left. Within its confines are the remains of the Bell Chapel. Dating from 1612, this was the parish church when the Rev. Patrick Brontë came from Hartshead in 1815. It was here that all but his eldest child were baptised. An old inscribed tablet incorporated into the ruin of the gable end tells *'this chappell was builded by freemason in the year of* our Lord 1612'. Two other salvaged datestones also feature. Most striking is the cupola that graced the tower, but is now at ground level. **Cross the road to St. James' church.** The 'new' parish church replaced the one that the Rev. Brontë knew later in the Victorian era.

The Bell Chapel remains, Thornton (with the present church behind)

Take a snicket immediately after the church, up onto Brontë Old Road. Going left, it becomes the one-way Market Street to enter the old village proper. Passed on the left is the Kipping Chapel: rebuilt in 1843, its predecessor was attended by the 'Thornton Dissenters' in Patrick Brontë's time. **Numerous shops, pubs and interesting old cobbled ways radiate, but the feature of greatest interest is the plaque that identifies the former parsonage, numbers 72 and 74.**

Patrick Brontë, his wife Maria and their eldest two children spent just five years here, yet in that time all four of their to-be-famous offspring were born: Charlotte in 1816, (Patrick) Branwell in 1817, Emily Jane in 1818 and Anne in 1820. The father himself found time to have two books published during his incumbency at Thornton, and no doubt planted the seed for what lay ahead. In recent times the house has been returned to the style of the Brontë era, and is open to the paying public during the summer months.

Continue on to where the road swings back down towards the main road, and here turn right up West Lane past the *Black Horse* pub. This slants steeply up to a junction with James Street. Head along a rough street, Reservoir View, virtually straight across. Just above is the *Sun Inn*. **Head along to a stile into fields at the end. The way runs a level course through several fields. Ignoring any branches it leads on (largely with a wall for company) to a kissing-gate into the extensive**

Thornton Cemetery. This grand section offers good views south over the valley and the viaduct, with Black Dyke chimney still on the skyline, and Ovenden Moor windfarm now directly ahead.

A broad surfaced pathway runs the length of the cemetery to another such gate at the far end. Pass along the rear of cottages to join a rough road, Close Head Lane. Turn right up it as far as a bend. One could go straight up here onto the road at Hill Top. **At this bend take a gap-stile on the left and head away with a crumbling wall. On through several similar crumbling walled fields, keep left at a solid wall with traces of the original embanked path. A couple of field tops further the way enters the yard at Close Head Farm.** Discernible in the fields below is the location of the southern entrance to Well Heads Tunnel, through which the railway burrowed 662 yards from Denholme. **Turn right up the short drive onto the road at Well Heads.** Just along to the right is the *White Horse Inn*.

The Way goes left, briefly, to the end of a long row of cottages where a tight gap-stile admits to a field. Bear sharp left to a wall-stile. Ahead is the spire of Denholme's 19th century church, with the mill village set back to the right. **The path strikes an obvious course through the fields to isolated Morton Farm.** Down to the right is Doe Park Reservoir, a popular sailing centre, with extensive Rombalds Moor on the skyline. **A stile to the left of an outhouse admits to the farm drive.**

Take a stile/gate a few yards up to the left of the buildings, and slant down the field to find a stile beneath a telegraph pole. Continue slanting down to a stile just above the corner opposite, then simply head along the wallside through several stiles to emerge by the head of colourful Denholme Clough. The path winds round to the left to descend to meet a path in the environs of Denholme Beck, in front of some cottages. From a stile on the left an enclosed path runs upstream to emerge onto their drive, continuing up onto the A644 Brighouse-Denholme road. There are two pubs and a bakery with a teashop at the busy crossroads at Keelham two minutes to the left.

Go left a short way on the footway and turn right up Cragg Lane. Almost at once a path turns right up a very narrow snicket, passing between houses to rise into a field. Swing up to the left with a wall on the right, and from a stile at a cross-wall continue up a flagged wallside path onto the A629 Halifax-Keighley road at Denholme Gate. Cross and go left a few yards to turn up Black Edge Lane.

Enclosed by walls throughout its length, this rough lane remains the uncomplicated course for a good mile and a half, rising gradually to Thornton Moor. Increasingly extensive views feature Ovenden Moor windfarm to the left and a stunning panorama far to the north. Distantly, a clear day reveals mighty Ingleborough rising above Oakworth Moor, flanked by numerous other tops of the Yorkshire Dales including Penyghent, some 30 miles distant. Quite a contrast with the receding metropolis of Bradford behind us! **Striding on beneath the unseen waters of Thornton Moor Reservoir, the way eventually becomes surfaced at a reservoir house. Ignore a branch right and go a little further to a junction with Sawood Lane.** The isolated *Dog & Gun* pub is five minutes down to the right through Sawood, but carries the penalty of a stiff climb to regain the route.

Bear left on the surfaced reservoir road. A stunning view now reveals the Brontë heartland, with Leeming Reservoir below, Oxenhope in the valley, and a rolling moorland scene behind, rising to Withins Height. **As the road turns into the reservoir grounds, an improving track runs on through a gate and onto moorland.** Ahead are the remains of quarry workings on Nab Hill, with its large cairn prominent. **After 250 yards, the track swings left at a wall corner. Here the Brontë Way is sent down a grassy sunken way on the right. This winds down to the right between old walls. At the bottom, in front of a scant ruin, go left a few yards and resume downhill between the remains of enclosing walls. At the bottom is a ladder-stile and the crossing of a water conduit.** This is part of a labyrinthine gathering system extending round the head of Oxenhope's valley.

Continue faintly down to a gap-stile and down a field centre. At the bottom keep on with a sturdy wall before dropping to a stile as wooded Stony Hill Clough comes in from the left. Advance a little further down to join an enclosed track. Turn left over the bridge and out into a green pasture, with Leeming Reservoir just to the right now. At an inflowing stream at the foot of the larger clough of Nan Scar, turn down to a wooden footbridge by the reservoir wall, and then up to the right with the wall.

The reservoir of 1877 makes a good foreground to the settlement of Leeming, dominated by its former mill. **From a stile at the top the path swings away from the reservoir, running on through several stiles to join a farm drive. This drops down through the fields to another farm road at the corner of the dam.** The *Lamb Inn* is two minutes away, across on the road. **The Brontë Way crosses straight over the farm road, dropping down a green way to the side of a house. Turn down the front onto a rough lane, a pleasing corner as it bridges the beck and runs on to meet Jew Lane at Back Leeming. Continue down here to the foot of Denholme Road on the edge of Oxenhope. Go left along Station Road as far as a crossroads by the Post office.**

Oxenhope is a fine example of a Pennine mill community. The village sits in a basin with steep hills rising on almost all sides, through pastures to the layer of moor above. While its illustrious neighbour Haworth draws the tourists, Oxenhope takes a back seat and seems quite happy to stay largely unaltered. More recent changes, however, have seen old mills torn down and replaced by modern housing. The squat church looks down from a lofty perch, witnessing, among other things, the July straw race, a now-famous annual event. This colourful pub crawl is also a great charity fund-raiser. The village centre pub is the *Bay Horse*.

St. Mary the Virgin, Oxenhope

Turn right along Yate Lane. This narrow back road passes the Manor House on the left, with mullioned windows at front and rear, and a water trough of 1859 on the right outside Yate House. **Keep on to the very end, and at the T-junction turn down narrow Dark Lane to emerge onto the A6033 Keighley-Hebden Bridge road. Cross and go down Harry Lane.** This earns the first view of the infamous Brow Moor wind turbine, the first in the area in 1992 and happily not yet joined by any colleagues. **Oxenhope railway station is just ahead.** This is the terminus of the Keighley & Worth Valley Railway, with a museum adjacent. British Railways made the five-mile line from Keighley redundant in 1961, but enthusiasts quickly stepped in to save it: today it is one of the country's most enduring steam railways, with lovingly restored stations and numerous special events throughout the year. Refreshments are normally available at the station.

The Brontë Way doesn't go as far as the station. Instead, as Harry Lane becomes Mill Lane, turn right along a rough road. The road quickly ends at a house with an inscription of 1823 above the door. An inviting footpath takes over, running alongside Bridgehouse Beck to a footbridge. Across, turn up onto the railway. Cross with care to a path slanting left up to a stile in the wall above. Climb the wallside to the houses, emerging via a stile/gate into the yard. That on the left is Bents House, which featured as Three Chimneys, home of 'The Railway Children' in the classic film set in the valley.

Head directly away on the straight drive rising onto Marsh Lane in the scattered hamlet of Marsh. The quickest way into Haworth turns right here. **The Way turns briefly left, then right up Old Oxenhope Lane.** The house on the corner is Marshlands, where Arthur Bell Nichols stayed prior to his marriage to Charlotte Brontë in 1854. Note also the facade of Old Oxenhope Hall hidden in foliage on the left. **At the bend at the top, step into the yard at the rear of Old Oxenhope Farm, then left up the wallside. Over the wall is an old millpond.**

Sections of old causey protrude as the way joins a farm track through a gate/stile and rising to the brow. Here locate a stile on the left admitting to a narrow, short-lived enclosed green way. At the end resume on the left side of the wall. Ahead is a big view down the length of the Worth Valley, with Oakworth to the left and Haworth Brow nearer to hand. Intriguingly, Haworth itself stays cleverly hidden from view. At the far end of the Worth Valley are the houses of Riddlesden beneath Rivock Edge and the Rombalds Moor skyline. Across to the right the solitary wind turbine overlooks a large sandstone quarry, while directly behind us many of the Ovenden Moor brethren are now breaking the skyline.

Keep on to reach Hole Farm, with its modern additions alongside. While the path strictly drops down past the buildings and climbs

away up the drive, an easier, higher level wall-side path runs on to meet the drive. From a stile almost opposite, a path heads invitingly across the field again towards Sowdens at the end. The siting of a modern urban street light in the field here will arouse curiosity: note also the sundial on the house side. **From the corner, the path turns into a narrow snicket to descend and zigzag along to a junction of ways above Haworth car park. It is to this point that the Way returns after being lured into Haworth.** Witnessing in disbelief the Japanese lettering on the footpath sign (there are more to follow, on the next stage), the unseen heart of the village is just two minutes ahead.

Advancing on solid flags, it is only as we are upon it that the parish church appears in front. An iron kissing-gate admits to the churchyard. The Brontë Parsonage is just up to the left, while the flagged path to the right leads down to the church gate and the top of the Main Street, hub of Haworth activity.

Haworth ceased to be just another village in the 19th century when the fame of the Brontës spread, though it took until relatively recently to become a full blown tourist honeypot. Focal point is the cobbled main street, lined with shops and climbing steeply to St. Michael's parish church. Fairly well surrounded by pubs, only the tower would be recognisable to the Brontës, the rest having been rebuilt around 1880. Inside, the Brontë Vault holds the remains of all but Anne, whose grave can be found overlooking the sea at Scarborough. It is said some 40,000 villagers are at rest in Haworth churchyard.

Hidden behind the church is the Parsonage, an elegant Georgian building of 1779. The right-hand (north) wing was added since Patrick Brontë's time by his successor, the Rev. John Wade in 1872. Just across the cobbled side street is the old school, where two of the sisters and Branwell taught. The Parsonage is now a museum of its former occupants, very much the spiritual heart of the Brontë scene. A comprehensive Brontë-themed shop is attached at the rear. Only minutes away is the open moorland that so inspired the sisters, while back down the main street is Haworth's second major attraction, the preserved steam railway. Although Haworth is at neither terminus, its station, with its goods yard, is at the hub of things. Interestingly, the railway actually leaves the Worth Valley near Oakworth to follow Bridgehouse Beck past Haworth to Oxenhope, a reminder of its original purpose, to serve the mills. Haworth has its own youth hostel, half a mile from the rail station off the B6142 Keighley road.

HAWORTH TO WYCOLLER

Distance: 8½ miles/13½km

Map:
1:50,000
Landranger 103 - Blackburn & Burnley
Landranger 104 - Leeds, Bradford & Harrogate
(small section)
1:25,000
Outdoor Leisure 21 - South Pennines

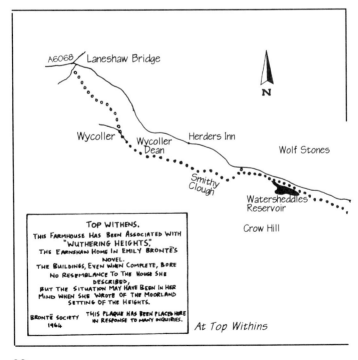

A6068 / Laneshaw Bridge

N

Wycoller

Wycoller Dean

Herders Inn

Wolf Stones

Smithy Clough

Watersheddles Reservoir

Crow Hill

TOP WITHENS.
THIS FARMHOUSE HAS BEEN ASSOCIATED WITH
"WUTHERING HEIGHTS",
THE EARNSHAW HOME IN EMILY BRONTË'S
NOVEL.
THE BUILDINGS, EVEN WHEN COMPLETE, BORE
NO RESEMBLANCE TO THE HOUSE SHE
DESCRIBED,
BUT THE SITUATION MAY HAVE BEEN IN HER
MIND WHEN SHE WROTE OF THE MOORLAND
SETTING OF THE HEIGHTS.

BRONTË SOCIETY
1964
THIS PLAQUE HAS BEEN PLACED HERE
IN RESPONSE TO MANY INQUIRIES.

At Top Withins

➡️ **From the front of the church, leave the Main Street by way of the flagged path to the left across the churchyard (the route of entry), leaving the churchyard behind and rising past allotments. At a T-junction above the car park, leave the inward route and turn right up a broader way, rising past the house at Balcony to emerge onto Dimples Lane on the edge of Penistone Hill. Cross straight over and bear left on the signposted path through the heather.**

Penistone Hill has changed from man's workshop to his playground. It is designated a country park, its former quarries now put to use as car parks for the leisure seeker. With its grand views of the Worth Valley and the heather moors beyond, this is as far as most visitors will venture. Most of the numerous guideposts over the next hour or so feature Japanese, an indication of the fascination for the Brontës with students from the Land of the Rising Sun. More sceptical observers see it as merely a gimmick that has earned extensive publicity for the area!

Good views look over the valley to the settlements of Oldfield, Pickles Hill and Oakworth, and back over Keighley to Rombalds Moor. The Brontë moorlands increasingly feature ahead, from Withins Height round above Stanbury to Wycoller Ark; Lower Laithe Reservoir is below. **Running broadly on, keep right at a signposted fork and the main path runs on towards old quarry spoil at the far end, culminating in a parking area.** The more distant Ponden Reservoir is seen ahead, while the attractive village of Stanbury occupies the crest of a ridge between Sladen Beck and the Worth Valley, making it easily identified in local views.

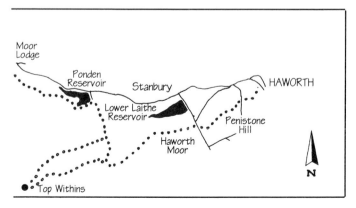

Haworth church

Keep right here, and very quickly the Way is signed down to the right at a track junction, now as a thinner path slanting down to cross unfenced Moorside Lane. Just up to the left, on the brow, is Tom Stell's Seat, a hoary gritstone block inscribed with the name of a local rambler 'who loved these moors'. **The path continues across the road, winding down to join a rough road at a cattle-grid. Turn left on this to march along the edge of Haworth Moor.** Haworth Moor is part of the South Pennine Moors Site of Special Scientific Interest, and is internationally renowned for its breeding birds.

Lower Laithe Reservoir from Penistone Hill

The rough road runs unfailingly on above abandoned farms in the fields below. Lower Laithe Reservoir was the culprit, as water boards cleared folk from the land to avoid contamination. **The way narrows into a broad path as the moor opens out.** The isolated farmstead of Harbour Lodge is seen ahead, but more stirring is the Top Withins skyline, its pair of attendant trees aiding identification as they just break the horizon. This is the true heart of the walk; the Pennine crossing and the Brontë heartland. **Across to the right is the colourful side valley of South Dean Beck, into which the Way is about to descend. The rougher path runs down and on to arrive at Brontë Bridge.**

Brontë Bridge

The Brontë Bridge is an attractive clapper-type bridge, but the equally famed Brontë Waterfall pushes the literary connection a little too far. It occurs on the tiny beck crossed just before the bridge, a slender trickle no different from a thousand other tinkling Pennine streams. By the path immediately before it is the stone known for obvious reasons as the Brontë Chair, while another boulder carries a brass plaque bearing a biblical quote. A boulder by the bridge bears a stone tablet, recording its re-building in 1990 following severe flash floods the previous spring.

Cross the bridge and head up the path directly behind, passing through an old wall and rising to a kissing-gate in a fence. Here the ways fork, with the literary pilgrimage option bearing left. Both routes are described overleaf. The detour is not an out-and-back walk, as a different return route (the mighty Pennine Way, no less) rejoins the Brontë Way further along: the detour involves an additional 2¼ miles, so it is wise to set aside an extra hour for this break from the main route.

Wuthering Heights

To incorporate a visit to Top Withins, take the left-hand path which rises a little more before running through a series of collapsed walls and the occasional intact one. The path remains clear throughout, and beyond a tiny beck it makes a short, steep climb to join the Pennine Way at the ruin of Withins. Go left on it for a brief pull to the more famous ruins of Top Withins. This is regarded as the Earnshaw home in Emily's classic *Wuthering Heights*.

Top Withins, or simply 'Withins' (as Withins and Lower Withins are now only piles of stones), is a famous ruin where one requires solitude in order to imbibe the very real atmosphere. It is difficult to imagine that this lonely outpost was once a home, but whether or not Emily actually visualised Heathcliff here, one can readily imagine her story being enacted in this bleak and inhospitable moorland setting which is, indeed 'wuthering'. To rejoin the Brontë Way, return down the flagged Pennine Way, but this time remain on it as it encourages big strides across Stanbury Moor. Remain on the broad way down to the first house, Upper Heights, where keep left as the track forks. A short way below the next house, Lower Height Farm, a crossroads is reached with the Brontë Way: turn left and by-pass the next paragraph.

Top Withins

The Brontë Way bears right, rising to a guidepost and running a few yards right to the rubble that was once the farm of Virginia. The remains of this local landmark were dismantled in 1996 on safety grounds. **Rise a few yards to another guidepost then slant right on a part causeyed path to a ladder-stile into a green pasture. Head away briefly with the crumbling wall, then bear left on a faint path to another ladder-stile. This re-admits onto moorland, and a fine green path runs on across two Landrover tracks to a stile between enclosing walls. At the second track we are joined by the Pennine Way and those who enjoyed the literary diversion.**

A splendid green path runs on between walls to rapidly reach a fine edge overlooking the Ponden scene. This impressive prospect centres on Ponden Reservoir directly below, with farms and fields rising to Keighley Moor opposite. Over to the left is the deep Ponden Clough. **Descend the wallside path to a rough road, going briefly right by the house at Buckley Green then sharp left on the short-lived drive down to the houses at Buckley House. Just in front, take a stile on the right and descend a pleasant enclosed way, swinging left at the bottom as a rough lane to emerge past the farm at Rush Isles onto a surfaced road at a corner of Ponden Reservoir.** Just down to the right is Ponden Mill, a shop with refreshments.

Turn left on the road along the south shore of the reservoir. Directly ahead is Ponden Clough, with its lower reaches well wooded, a riot of colour culminating abruptly where two tumbling rocky becks merge. **At the end of the reservoir the road climbs to Ponden Hall.** Ponden Hall is a characterful structure perched high above the

reservoir. Emily visited the Heaton family here and portrayed the house as Thrushcross Grange, the Linton home in *Wuthering Heights*. Today it offers accommodation, including camping. An inscription above the door informs that the original house of 1634 was rebuilt in 1807.

Ponden Hall

A rough road climbs away from the hall. Keep straight on over the brow to descend to the rear of an enviably sited house. Below is the slender upper arm of the reservoir. A green path runs on above the house to a bend. As the Pennine Way turns sharp right down this green way, our way takes the stile in front and along a similar way. At Whitestone Farm the route is diverted left a few yards to a ladder-stile, then past the garden and on to regain its original course at the end. Just a little further turn up a few yards to a gateway on the right, and slant across a field to the far bottom corner.

A plank bridge on Whitestone Clough precedes a wallside climb to Old Snap. Keep left of the farmhouse and on a short grassy way to a brow, with the upper reaches of the Worth Valley below. From this point the Way follows a concession path to the Pennine watershed. Go left on the inviting green path along the bank top and crumbling wallside. At the end a gate admits to a green walled way, leading to a ladder-stile at the far end. Across the now narrow valley is the impressive facade of Moor Lodge, a Victorian shooting lodge currently operating as a fashionable pine retailer. High on the skyline behind are the Wolf Stones.

Marker posts guide the initially faint path down to enter the deeper confines of the infant river Worth, merely a small stream over the wall. A path then runs upstream. The bizarre surround of rhododendrons is a hangover from the heyday of Moor Lodge, nevertheless this is a very colourful quarter with bracken, scrub and a few rocks overlooking the stream. Although one or two moist moments feature, this really is a grand section. The confines narrow to reach a footbridge on the stream, our one contact with the Worth. The river runs a 10 mile course from Watersheddles to enter the river Aire beyond Keighley, and the little grassy bank makes a good spot to halt.

Resume upstream, the path encountering several stiles before rising steadily up the bank from a stile by a rowan tree. The path runs at mid height through a couple of old walls, and with the grassy dam of Watersheddles Reservoir appearing just ahead, a large boundary stone is reached. This was erected in 1985 to mark the Brontë Way's departure from God's Own Country into Lancashire.

From the ladder-stile beyond, the path slants up to a barn and on to a Brontë Way information board by the reservoir embankment. Over a ladder-stile a good path runs on through a strip of heather

alongside the water, parallel with the moorland road to Laneshaw Bridge. Crossing the stile brings Lancashire's most famous landmark (begging Blackpool Tower's pardon) into view, as Pendle Hill appears far beyond the reservoir head. The Wolf Stones break the moorland skyline much closer to hand up to the right. Watersheddles is an apt name for this Pennine watershed reservoir, which suffers a curious identity crisis. Though within Yorkshire's gathering grounds and belonging to Yorkshire Water, the errant wanderings of the county boundary mean it is actually located entirely within Lancashire.

At the end another stile exits the reservoir wall, and the path runs left outside the wall. Beyond the reservoir a fence takes over and we cross a shooters' track to a minor brow, which at 1148ft/350m marks the summit of the Brontë Way. Lancashire proper appears ahead, heralded by the mighty frame of Pendle Hill which will come to feature strongly as a backdrop to the latter stages of the Way.

Continue to a kissing-gate in the fence (which turns to shadow the adjacent road). Extensive rolling moors are spread all about now. This is the final chance to look back at the Ovenden Moor windfarm, a long-standing Brontë Way landmark that will not be missed. Crow Hill rises darkly to the south, with mighty Boulsworth Hill set further back to its right. **A firm path now runs on, encountering a side-stream and enjoying a short grassy spell before joining a Landrover track. This marks the end of the concessionary section. Turn down this initially enclosed byway into the head of Smithy Clough.** Pendle Hill makes a splendid backdrop to the extensive East Lancashire scene.

The rough road runs unfailingly down, crossing the stream by a stone arched bridge in the environs of the extensive grassy hummocks of Smithy Clough Scar, also known as Hilly Holes. These are hushings, the result of centuries-old limestone extraction. The 'alien' rock was deposited here by glaciers at the end of the Ice Age, some 10,000 years ago. The limestone boulders would be won by releasing water from dams formed by diverted streams, scouring the vegetation away in the process. The stone would be fired in kilns, and the resulting powder was most commonly used as a sweetener for spreading on the locally acidic moorland soils to improve them for cultivation.

The track swings left up to a brow and path junction at a three-way guidepost. This is an important decision point, as the true route of the Way makes for Wycoller.

Anyone omitting Wycoller (which would be a shame) can opt for the direct route, which at this point is also the Pendle Way. If omitting Wycoller, keep straight on the broad track, and with the following directions the Brontë Way will rejoin us within ten minutes. Continue along the firm track, though don't march blindly off along its obvious course ahead. Instead, after 100 yards bear right on a thin, reedy path by the wall. Beyond a gate in the corner it runs on more happily along the field top, becoming briefly enclosed before emerging into true open country beneath Brink Ends, a gaunt looking place. Rejoin the main narrative on page 44.

Boulsworth Hill from Foster's Leap, looking across Wycoller Dean

For Wycoller, pass through the stile/gate on the right and descend the reed-fringed track towards the deep side valley known as Wycoller Dean. Glorious views stretch far out over Pendle country to the big hill itself. Just over to the right, the skyline *Herders Inn* perches above the colourful rocky bank of Foster's Leap. **A pleasant descent through rough pasture leads down towards Smithy Clough, and at a stile/gate arrives beneath Parson Lee Farm.**

Ignoring a footbridge continue downstream on the drive, passing a lovely little waterfall in this charming beckside setting. The drive from Dean House Farm merges in tandem with two streams: this is the point to which the route returns on Stage 4, after leaving

Wycoller. For Wycoller keep straight on the rough lane, in the company of the stream to enter the hamlet. En route we pass the very old, single-slab Clam Bridge, by a ford - misleadingly looking precariously perched - and the footbridge of Copy House Bridge. The stream is a good place to observe dippers flying just above water level.

Wycoller is a fascinating hamlet of mullioned windowed cottages bypassed by the outside world since the Industrial Revolution failed to gain a foothold. It is difficult to believe that two centuries ago, several hundred people lived here. Handloom weaving was a major industry, but as the large mills sprang up, workers abandoned the place to take up employment in the towns. As a result Wycoller spent much of the 20th century largely derelict, but more recently its very isolation and untouched character have ensured its popularity.

Today it has its own country park administered by the Lancashire Countryside Service, visitors flock here, and all but the hall seems to be renovated. In open space stand the ruins of Wycoller Hall, a 16th century country house later extended by the last squire, Henry Cunliffe. It is thought to have been the Ferndean Manor of Charlotte's *Jane Eyre*. Alongside is an ancient clapper bridge, while a most characterful packhorse bridge of 13th century origin stands by a ford. The restored Aisled Barn was built in the 1630s to store grain, and was later used as a carriage house. Along with the old hall it is the focal point, and features a display including the area's weaving history (normally open at weekends). There is also a craft centre and refreshments.

• *Link route from Wycoller to the A6068 at Laneshaw Bridge, for Keighley-Colne-Burnley buses.* When the road crosses Laithe Hill Bridge before leaving the hamlet, turn immediately down a rough road past a white-walled house with mullioned windows. The drive crosses Lowlands Bridge, and as it turns right to the Old Pump House, keep straight on the wallside. The path runs on a bank above the beck and enjoys a brief flagged section before reaching a stile at the end. Pass through and head left with the wall and side-stream. Cross an intervening stile to arrive on the bank of Wycoller Beck. Turn right on a small bridge over the side-stream, and the way is generally obvious, always on the bank above the meandering beck. At the end the path emerges onto a road alongside a row of cottages. Turn right to a junction, then left on the bridge over the little river Laneshaw to rise to the main road opposite the *Emmott Arms* in Laneshaw Bridge.

WYCOLLER to GAWTHORPE HALL

Distance: 14½ miles/23km

Map:
1:50,000
Landranger 103 - Blackburn & Burnley
1:25,000
Outdoor Leisure 21 - South Pennines

• *Link from the A6068 at Laneshaw Bridge to Wycoller.* From the *Emmott Arms* cross the main road and head down School Lane to cross the bridge on the modest river Laneshaw. Turn immediately right on Carriers Row, passing a former chapel. After a row of cottages, take a kissing-gate on the left and head away, a clear path running through the fields. With Wycoller Beck close by on the right, the green path runs upstream, always on the bank above the meandering beck. After a small bridge over a side-stream, the path deserts the beck and

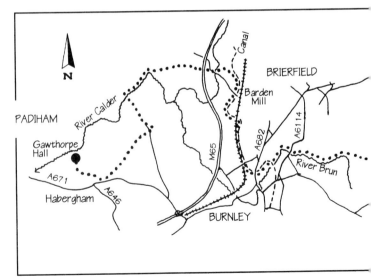

rises left, crossing an intervening stile then resuming with wall and side-stream. At the top the path turns sharp right, a short flagged section by the wall preceding arrival high above the beck. Advance along the wallside, passing the Old Pump House and merging into its drive to run along into Wycoller by way of Lowlands Bridge, and joining the road at Laithe Hill Bridge.

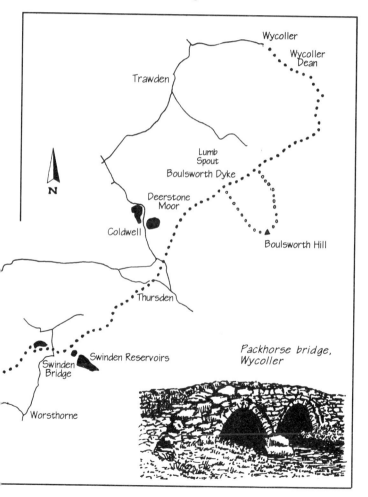

Packhorse bridge, Wycoller

To leave Wycoller, head upstream on the road from the hall and barn, as a traffic-free byway in tandem with the stream. This happy arrangement is maintained through Wycoller Dean as far as the confluence and fork to which the previous stage of the Brontë Way descended. En route we pass the historic, single-slab Clam Bridge, with a ford alongside. There is also a glimpse of examples of vaccary walling in fields up to the left, an old style of field boundary consisting of upright slabs (a vaccary was a cattle farm). **At this waymarked fork rise right, on the drive to Dean House Farm.** This section enjoys fine views of the rocky environs of Foster's Leap over to the left.

Vaccary walls, Wycoller, looking to Pendle Hill

At Dean House Farm go straight on through the yard to the gate at the far end. Pass through another gate just beyond, and up a grassy track with a wall on the right. Ahead, set back to the right, stretches the broad frame of Boulsworth Hill. **As the wall disappears continue straight up to a ladder-stile onto a broad, reedy walled way. Cross to the far wall and turn right on a thin path. This is another junction of Ways, for here we re-unite with the Pendle Way, this time for a longer spell, and it brings the 'omitting Wycoller' route with it.** Grand views remain with us throughout the ensuing long strides.

Between diverging walls keep straight on, the way descending to a gate in a wall before crossing the deep Turnhole Clough. Up the other bank an old boundary stone is passed as the path rises gently away, upstream through increasingly colourful terrain. The many contours of Boulsworth Hill now entirely dominate this fine surround of rolling moorland. Some good sections of stone causey testify to the history of this old packhorse route, and several of them incorporate benchmarks. Note that this route is a permissive bridleway, popular with mountain bikers.

In the company of little Saucer Hill Clough, a lengthy section with a sturdy wall leads to the brow of the hill, and the path descends to a junction with a surfaced road. Followed right, this would lead down to Trawden, for buses to Colne and linking paths to Wycoller. **Keep straight on along the base of the moor to the barns at Spoutley Lumb.** This is the location of two potential detours, one easy, one more strenuous.

Lumb Spout

The easy option adds on a gentle half-hour as it drops down to visit the waterfall of Lumb Spout. From a ladder-stile on the right just before the barns, head down the wallside. From a stile at the bottom, continue down by a few trees to approach a stream. Turn left downstream, briefly, to suddenly reach a superb vantage point for the shady hollow enclosing Lumb Spout. The nearby cottage named on the map is just a pile of rubble.

Boulsworth Hill

The more ambitious detour is a looping concession path climbing to the summit of Boulsworth Hill. This two mile, elongated horseshoe rejoins the Brontë Way a mere half-mile along the main route. The way begins easily enough, up a waterworks access road. However this is soon relinquished as the path forges uphill, marker posts confirming the fairly obvious route. Eventually the broad ridge is joined at Little Chair Stones, and the path swings right to cross the broad top to the waiting Ordnance Survey column.

Boulsworth Hill rises as an upturned boat from the rolling moorland, and its lengthy top bristles with an assortment of gritstone outcrops. The summit, Lad Law, is itself a cluster of boulders, and at 1696ft/517m this is one of the principal summits of the South Pennines. Our moorland spell above the intake wall is enjoyed courtesy of the water company, which has deigned to allow the public a narrow access strip. Don't forget to pay those water rates! Boulsworth's greatest asset as a viewpoint is its 360° panorama. A good half-hour could be passed identifying the many hills and moors, which include those of the Yorkshire Dales, the Lake District, Bowland and the Peak District.

Return on the clear path heading west, initially moist but quickly reaching a scattering of boulders around the Abbot Stone. From this fine location the ground steepens, and the path transforms into a grassy, surprisingly peat-free way. The last stage accompanies a wall down to rejoin the track, turning left.

Forge on along the farm road to Boulsworth Dyke. By this stage a clear day will reveal Ingleborough, Whernside and Penyghent, the famous Three Peaks of Yorkshire, many miles to the north-west. **The broad track continues across streams that form a colourful clough immediately to the right. The Boulsworth path returns and the track climbs to a brow just beyond the top end of a plantation not shown on current maps.**

At 1125ft/343m this is the highest point of the Wycoller-Gawthorpe section, and a recumbent boundary stone rests alongside. The superb Dales panorama has extended eastwards from the Three Peaks, bringing in the Upper Wharfedale giants of Buckden Pike and Great Whernside. Boulsworth Hill finally leaves our thoughts as Pendle Hill takes over to the west, while Great Hamelden is also prominent to the south of Burnley. Closer to hand, the Coldwell Reservoirs appear ahead.

The Way begins a gentle descent across Deerstone Moor, and here be sure to locate a waymark as the less obvious Brontë Way strikes off left from the possibly more appealing course of the Pendle Way. This other route, incidentally, drops down to the Coldwell Reservoirs: don't feel you're missing out on the delights of the Coldwell Inn, as indicated on some maps: apparently notorious for gambling and cockfighting, it closed in 1939 and is now put to use as a residential centre, principally for the handicapped. It has a tearoom, toilets and visitor information.

The Brontë Way runs a slimmer course, sometimes moistly across rough moor grass to a simple bridge and a stile. Continue across better terrain to another such bridge, slant up the steep bank and along to a curious stone arch. This porchway is all that remains of New House Farm, and in this isolated spot makes a fine landmark. Two inscriptions feature on stone tablets, each making reference to the building's origins in 1672, and its original occupants Robert Parker and his family. Lingering here awhile, there is a surprising absence of evidence of the proximity of several large towns, merely a good mixture of fields, farms, moors, walls, and even distant peaks.

The thin path continues on to a stile/gate beyond, then cross a pasture to another stile/gate onto a corner of open ground. Advance the few yards to the narrow road, and turn briefly left to footpath signs at the corner of Thursden Wood. Ahead is a fine new prospect, that of the Thursden Valley, at our feet. **There is a choice of ways down to the road below, for the Brontë Way ignores the public footpath and takes a less than obvious concessionary route through the wood.**

*The concessionary path turns down into the wood just a few yards further, on a flight of wooden steps that were obliterated by contractors' work on the last visit. The path drops down, bearing left as yellow painted bands on tree trunks help confirm the route. It swings down to a ladder-stile out of the trees, going left a few yards on a short track to join another quiet road coming down off the moor into the unsung Thursden Valley. This is the first meeting with the Burnley Way.

*The public footpath crosses the stile into the field to descend colourful terrain outside the trees, some moist moments being avoided by foraging onto the adjacent characterful spur. The path hugs the woodland fence to descend into undergrowth, emerging via a stile into the farmyard at Thursden. Turning right, the drive leads out past the house and down to the road.

Turn right for a few minutes, leaving the road as it starts to climb. From a stile on the left gain the bank of Thursden Brook and head away, through a pasture becoming enclosed by stream and wall to reach a footbridge in a lovely setting. Across, a path slants up through trees to a stile in the old wall/fence. Climbing directly up the wallside out of Park Wood the Ways part company, for now, as ours keeps straight on up to a gap at the top. A good path then rakes up to the right, an old quarrymens' way beneath recolonised spoilheaps. Look back for a good view over the well wooded Thursden Valley, backed by a moorland skyline.

On the brow turn left to rise to a ladder-stile across the field, and joining a surfaced farm road, go left. This slight rise leads to another high point at 1072ft/327m. Immediately on the right is the rounded grassy knoll of Pike Low, an ancient burial mound. Ahead, meanwhile, are grand views to the moorland south of Burnley, featuring Thieveley Pike, with the Cliviger Gorge fronting the Forest of Rossendale. Just ahead is the village of Worsthorne. Looking back north, meanwhile, Ingleborough, Penyghent, Buckden Pike and Great Whernside are still on show. By the way, it's almost downhill (or at least level) all the way now! **The drive quickly descends to Sweetwell House Farm.**

On entering the yard take a stile to the left of two gates, into a field. With a deep-cut side clough below, go right with the wall, and an improving way winds down to a ladder-stile and old gate at the end. A grassy old way slants down the pasture between long crumbled walls, crossing the marshy environs of the stream at the bottom. Ignoring stiles in the wall, keep on with it past wooden sheds to approach the smaller of the Swinden Reservoirs. Passing beneath power lines the path drops to a pair of stiles/gates to emerge onto a surfaced drive from Ing Hey. Go left on this as it winds down the field to join the road at Swinden Bridge.

There is a splendid chance to break journey here, as one minute up to the right stands the imposing *Roggerhamgate Inn*. In the other direction, the village of Worsthorne is a short mile away. **The route crosses straight over into a pleasant, walled green way alongside Lee Green Reservoir.** Completed in 1876, this small sheet of water is more pleasing than most in its leafy setting. **Cross the dam at the end to a wall-stile, and turn downstream. The Burnley Way rejoins at this point. A good path run down through undergrowth into the woodland of Houghton Hagg, a truly delightful section in the valley of Swinden Water.**

Forge on through the trees and a mini-ravine, perhaps enjoying one or two bluebell patches, or later in the year merely bracken. At a minor fork keep right, with open fields just further right. Running a gauntlet of hollies, the path passes out of the wood at a stile, but remains along the edge of the trees. Just past an early footbridge a guidepost sends the path left towards the stream, then right to resume downstream in more open country. Just one factory spoils the skyline ahead, otherwise we could still be anywhere. **The way runs straight on across a vast sloping pasture, some way across which a stile re-admits to the wooded environs of the stream. Advance on to pass a footbridge above a weir.**

The river Brun (which gave Burnley its name) comes in on the left, and just beyond, the path emerges onto a rough road with a confluence just ahead at Netherwood Bridge. Once more the Burnley Way parts company, but the Brontë Way keeps straight on the rough, wide road downstream. This leads on through trees to a big factory on the right. When the road turns away, continue downstream on a path alongside allotments on the edge of the town of Burnley.

The path passes under a road bridge (A6114) to emerge into the urban environs of Bank Hall Park. Remain on the surfaced riverside path to pass under a canal aqueduct. Just through, double back right up a path to gain the towpath of the Leeds-Liverpool Canal. This runs a 127¼ mile course between its two great city termini, and is the northernmost of three trans-Pennine waterways. Unlike its counterparts further south, which tunnelled deep below the hills, this one took advantage of the low-level Aire Gap to breach the Pennines by way of a chain of locks. It fully opened in 1816 for what proved to be a relatively short-lived industrial use, being overtaken during the course of the 19th century by the arrival of the railways. Today it is a vibrant amenity catering for a wide range of leisure users.

Go left/north on the towpath, which negotiates an amenable course through this section of Burnley. The Industrial Revolution made Burnley the heart of the cotton mill country, and coal mines operated at numerous locations around the district. The arrival of the Leeds-Liverpool Canal was a boost to trade, and this at least survives today with its highlight being a mile-long embankment 60 feet above the town centre. A circuitous detour south along the towpath leads to the town centre and the Weavers' Triangle at Burnley Wharf, a fascinating area of Victorian mills and associated buldings, with a visitor centre.

The first road bridge we pass under is the A682, from which the town centre and railway station can be accessed. Beyond here are terraced houses and factories, and the recently landscaped recreational area of Byerden Holme. Bridges modern and traditional are encountered, both serving Byerden Holme, then the railway bridges the canal. Modern housing and a bridleway bridge precede another road bridge at Barden Mill (millshop and tearoom). The canal suddenly bursts into true open countryside, and a broader path leads to the next little bridge. With Pendle Hill looking good directly ahead, this is the point to leave the canal. Note that Brierfield rail station is just a mile from here, by continuing to the next bridge then up over the canal and up a lane onto the A682.

Ignoring the bridge, turn down to a stile to the left, and a thin path slants right, down the field to another stile. The M65 motorway is just ahead now. With two paths signed, it is simplest to head straight down the thin path past the bushes, then veer left above the sizeable Pendle Water to a thin path on a steep bank above the river. Go left briefly to a kissing-gate onto Barden Lane, the Burnley-Fence road.

New in Pendle Bridge

Turn right over New in Pendle Bridge, immediate left at Wood End, then sharp right up the front of the short row of houses. From the stile at the top, rise up the field to approach the M65. A pair of neighbouring stiles give access to our own footbridge high above the motorway. Opened in 1988, the M65 - the East Lancs Motorway - was for many years the 'road to nowhere', for at neither end did it link to the motorway network. 1997 brought that to an end, with the completion of the western extension around Blackburn. The more controversial eastern end, however, has seen several options floated, with at the very least major continuations, if not motorway standard, running either to Skipton or South Craven. Only time will tell whether it remains a dead-end...

The path drops down to the right into a field. Rise up the hedge-side, quickly crossing a footbridge to its other side. Resume along several field-sides to drop down at the end to a footbridge over the foot of Spurn Clough. Directly up the bank behind, a surfaced access road is reached. Cross straight over this and across the vast field, locating a tiny footbridge in the folds ahead (left of a pylon) from where a clear path runs on the colourful bank.

At the end of the bank the path enters a wooded corner to meet the river Calder on a sharp bend. The river has recently been swelled by absorbing Pendle Water. **After a footbridge on a side-stream at the foot of Moor Isles Clough, the Way runs out into a large open pasture. On the flats by the river bear a little right, tracing the foot of the slope to arrive at a sturdy metal footbridge across the river.** At this point the Brontë, Burnley and Pendle Ways all meet.

Our Way crosses the bridge and heads away to a stile into a large field. A fine green way curves up the slope, passing a huge roofed barn at Hunters Oak on the left. Look back for a grand view of Pendle Hill rising above the fields. At the field top, Hagg Wood on the right is in the care of the Woodland Trust. **At a stile above, the foot of the surfaced Ightenhill Park Lane is joined. Rise up this past Hollins Farm and up to a cottage. Turn right on a narrow snicket immediately after, to emerge into a field.** This final open section enjoys glorious views over the green valley of the Calder to Pendle Hill.

Head away along the tops of two fields, with Habergham's church spire appearing ahead. A rough track forms to lead on to the farm buildings of Top o' th' Close. Pass left of the big cattle barn to a stile admitting to the yard. Pass between the two houses and out on the drive, with modern housing on the left. At the end cross straight over a back road (Cornfield Grove) and down an enclosed green way to emerge onto the A671 Burnley-Padiham road at Habergham.

Turn right. At the junction just ahead are the parish church (All Saints with John the Baptist), a shop and a pub, the *George IV*. Its old Duttons windows recall a Blackburn brewery that fell victim to 1960s takeover mania. Nearest rail station (Rose Grove) is under a mile distant, left on Kiddrow Lane at the traffic lights. **The Brontë Way concludes by advancing just as far as a lodge, where the Way is signposted along the long Habergham Drive into the grounds of Gawthorpe Hall, finishing right in front of the old house itself. Well done!**

Gawthorpe Hall dates back to the early 1600s, having been the home of the Shuttleworth family, first recorded in the area way back in 1388. Colonel Sir Richard Shuttleworth successfully led local men in the Parliamentarian cause in a nearby Civil War skirmish, and many succeeding generations served in Parliament. Marriage of the heiress Janet to the educationalist Dr. James Kay in 1842 brought changes, including the restoration of the old house. Later becoming Sir James

and Lady Kay-Shuttleworth, they befriended Charlotte Brontë who first visited here in 1850. Indeed, it was after a spell here that the recently married Charlotte took ill, an illness that was to see her onto her death bed. Tragically, two members of the family were to perish in each of the two World Wars. Rachel Kay-Shuttleworth was the last of the family to reside here, and her consuming interest in needlework left a fine legacy, a celebrated collection of textiles. A National Trust property since 1970, it is administered by Lancashire County Council, and also features a shop and tearoom. The house is open afternoons from April to October (not Monday or Friday), the grounds all year.

Outstanding among the outbuildings is the Great Barn, built at the same time as the house. Such is its size that it spent a quarter-century in use by the 'Clarets' - Burnley Football Club - for indoor practice! The team's training ground is still close by. The hall's grounds are attractively laid out, from the neat lawn at the front to the rose garden at the rear. All around is lovely greenery, crowned by some outstanding beech trees. The river Calder flows by wooded banks immediately below the grounds, while Pendle Hill forms a suitable backdrop.

Gawthorpe Hall

A LOG OF THE WALK

Date	Place	Road	Miles stage	total	Notes
	Oakwell Hall	A652	-	-	
	Red House, Gomersal	A651	1¼	1¼	
	Royds Park, Rawfolds	A638	2¾	2¾	
	Hightown, Liversedge	A649	3¾	3¾	
	Hartshead Church	B6119	4¾	4¾	
	Bailiff Bridge	A641	7½	7½	
	Norwood Green		8¾	8¾	
	Shelf	A6036	10½	10½	
	Clayton Heights	A647	2	12½	
	Thornton Church	B6145	3¾	14¼	
	Denholme Gate	A629	6¼	16¾	
	Oxenhope	A6033	9½	20	
	Haworth	B6142	11½	22	
	Ponden Reservoir		3½	25½	
	Watersheddles Resr.		5½	27½	
	Wycoller		8½	30½	
	Boulsworth Dyke		2½	33	
	Thursden		4¾	35¼	
	Swinden Bridge		6¾	37¼	
	Burnley	A6114	9	39½	
	Burnley	A682	9½	40	
	New in Pendle Bridge		11¼	41¾	
	Habergham	A671	14	44½	
	Gawthorpe Hall	A671	14½	45	

The Country Code
- Respect the life and work of the countryside
- Protect wildlife, plants and trees
- Keep to public paths across farmland
- Safeguard water supplies
- Go carefully on country roads
- Keep dogs under control
- Guard against all risks of fire
- Fasten all gates • Leave no litter - take it with you
- Make no unnecessary noise
- Leave livestock, crops and machinery alone
- Use gates and stiles to cross fences, hedges and walls

INDEX

Principal features

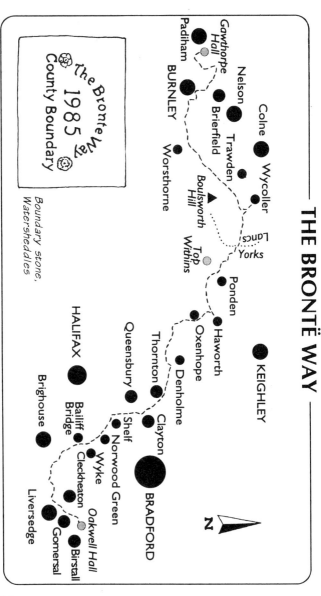

THE BRONTË WAY

The Brontë Way
1985
County Boundary

Boundary stone,
Watersheddles

Padiham
Gawthorpe Hall
BURNLEY
Nelson
Brierfield
Colne
Trawden
Wycoller
Worsthorne
Boulsworth Hill
Top Withins
Lancs
Yorks
Ponden
HALIFAX
Queensbury
Thornton
Oxenhope
Haworth
Denholme
KEIGHLEY
Brighouse
Bailiff Bridge
Shelf
Clayton
Norwood Green
Wyke
Cleckheaton
BRADFORD
Liversedge
Oakwell Hall
Gomersal
Birstall

N